Table of Contents

Shadows Unveiled

Into the Digital Abyss

Ghost in the Machine

Echoes of Vengeance

Shadows and Synapses

Web of Shadows

The Architect's Shadow

Shadows Within Shadows

Shadows Cast by Hidden Light

Shadows of Truth

Whispers in the Winds of Change

Echoes of Resolution

Shadows Upon the Web

Shadows Unearthed

Echoes of the Unseen

Betrayal in the Shadows

Veils of Betrayal and Illumination

Shadows of Allegiance

Tides of Betrayal and Awakening

Veils of Shadow and Light

Veils Lifted

Whispers of the Viper

Shadows Turned Allies

In the Shadows of Betrayal

Alliances Unbound

Whispers of the Gale

Winds of Change

The Turn of the Tides

The Unveiling

Chains of Shadows, Tears in the Market

Navigating the Path Out of Trafficking

by

Dr. ant

Although the author and publisher have made every effort to ensure that the information in this book was correct at press time, the author and publisher do not assume and hereby disclaim any liability to any party for any loss, damage, or disruption caused by errors or omissions, whether such errors or omissions result from negligence, accident, or any other cause.

This publication is designed to provide accurate and authoritative information with regard to the subject matter covered. It is sold with the understanding that the publisher is not engaged in rendering professional services. If legal advice or other expert assistance is required, the services of a competent professional should be sought.

The fact that an organization or website is referred to in this work as a citation and/or a potential source of further information does not mean that the author or the publisher

Chains of Shadows, Tears in the Market: Navigating the Path Out of Trafficking

Contents

Chapter 1: Shadows on the Horizon

The streets of Staten Island were alive with the cacophony of daily hustle, the air thick with anticipation and unrest. Amidst this tapestry of urban life, Detective Laura Henley moved with purpose, her keen eyes missing nothing. Her reputation in the NYPD as a shrewd and determined officer was well-earned, fortified by years of battling the city's underbelly. Today, however, something new had caught her attention, a case that would not only test her resolve but align her destiny with two remarkable individuals.

The story of Sofia Rodriguez, a seventeen-year-old girl who had endured and survived the harrowing ordeal of human trafficking, had come to Laura's notice. The tale was one of unimaginable suffering, resilience, and a desperate cry for freedom that resonated with Laura's own sense of justice. It was also a story that intertwined Sofia's fate with Christopher Viento, a man whose profound compassion and unique insights into the human psyche had already begun to alter the course of the investigation.

Christopher, a retired mental health doctor turned vigilant guardian, had taken Sofia under his wing, offering guidance and protection. His experience in the psychiatric field provided him with an unparalleled understanding of the traffickers' motivations and strategies. But this very insight, coupled with his relentless pursuit of justice, had painted a target on both Christopher and Sofia. Their adversaries were shrouded in the shadows of society's apathy, making the duo's journey to safety and vindication all the more perilous.

Laura's resolve hardened as she considered the task ahead. Bringing down the traffickers who preyed on the vulnerable was no small feat, but she was undeterred. She knew that her skills, combined with Christopher's knowledge and Sofia's firsthand experience, could form a formidable force against the darkness that sought to engulf their lives. The detective made a silent vow to stand by their side, to fight for those who had no voice, and to bring light into the darkest of places.

As the day gave way to night, the alleys and backstreets of Staten Island whispered secrets of crimes unseen and voices unheard. But Laura, Christopher, and Sofia, each driven by their own demons and desires, were ready to confront the shadows head-on. It was a battle fraught with danger and uncertainty, yet it was one they were willing to wage for the sake of justice and redemption. The stage was set for a confrontation that would shake the very foundations of their world, a trial by fire that would either forge them stronger or consume them entirely.

Chapter 2: Beneath the Veil of Blue

As the curtain of night enfolded Staten Island, the trio, under the cloak of darkness, orchestrated their next move. Laura, with her detective instincts sharply honed, suspected a malignancy within her ranks that threatened to cripple their endeavors. The air buzzed with tension as she shared her suspicions with Christopher and Sofia, her voice barely a whisper amongst the whirring of invasive thoughts.

The revelation hit Sofia like a physical blow, a specter from her past given form. Among those implicated in Laura's findings was an officer who had once promised Sofia safety, only to betray her trust in the cruelest way imaginable. Faced with this ghost, the floodgates of memory swung wide open, unearthing the trauma that Sofia had fought so hard to bury. Yet, within the labyrinth of her fears, a spark of resilience flickered to life, igniting a resolve to confront her tormentor, to reclaim her narrative.

Christopher, ever the anchor in the storm, delved deeper into understanding the mind of their enemy. Connecting dots with the precision of a seasoned psychiatrist, he pieced together a psychological profile that was both illuminating and terrifying. His findings pointed to a network that was more extensive and entrenched than they had feared, a hydra with many heads, each feeding off the misery of the unsuspecting. Yet, in this dark tapestry, Christopher discerned a thread, a potential lead that could guide them to the heart of the operation.

The decision to act was unanimous, driven by a shared fury and an unwavering commitment to justice. The operation, risky and fraught with the potential for betrayal, was set into motion with meticulous care. Laura's law enforcement connections, Christopher's psychological insights, and Sofia's invaluable inside knowledge coalesced into a formidable strike force. The target was a fraction of the trafficking ring, a crucial domino that, if toppled, could initiate a cascade of downfall.

The night of the operation was a symphony of tension, every moment stretched taut with anticipation. As the team moved in, cloaked in the anonymity of the dark, the air was thick with the promise of confrontation. Sofia, her heart a battleground of fear and courage, faced the unfolding drama with a fierce determination. Christopher, his belief in the cause unshakeable, stood ready to lend his strength. And Laura, her spirit aflame with a righteous wrath, led the charge against those who would prey on the innocent.

The operation was a dance on the razor's edge, a flurry of shouts, shadows, and heart-stopping moments. In the end, the dust settled on a scene of chaotic victory. A significant blow had been dealt to the trafficking ring, but the victory was tinged with the knowledge of the battle yet to come. As they regrouped, their resolve hardened, ready to face the darkness with a light unyielding.

Chapter 3: Tangled Webs

The aftermath of the operation left the streets of Staten Island eerily quiet, as if the city itself held its breath. Among the dimly lit alleys and silent storefronts, Laura, Christopher, and Sofia regrouped, their hearts heavy with both triumph and trepidation. The victory was significant, yet it was merely a battle won in an ongoing war. The next phase of their mission would draw them into uncharted waters, testing their resolve like never before.

While sifting through the evidence gathered during the raid, a shocking discovery was made. Documents seized from the trafficking ring hinted at connections far beyond the criminal underworld, reaching into the echelons of political power. A high-profile political figure, revered by the public and positioned in a realm of untouchable authority, was implicated. The revelation sent ripples through the team, forcing them to question how deep the roots of corruption had spread.

The challenge before them grew exponentially. To expose this connection could topple towers of influence and provoke a storm of public outrage. But the path was fraught with peril. Surveillance operations to gather incontrovertible evidence saw the trio dancing on the knife's edge of danger. It was during one such operation that fate intervened, thrusting them into an unforeseen crisis. Sofia, positioned as the eyes on the ground, was nearly compromised by a sudden sweep of the area. It was only through Christopher's quick thinking and Laura's decisive actions that a dramatic rescue was executed, pulling Sofia from the jaws of catastrophe.

The narrow escape only served to steel their determination. The stakes had never been higher, propelling them toward a discovery that would expand the scope of the investigation beyond the borders of the city, hinting at an international network of traffickers. This global connection offered a daunting prospect, but also a pivotal opportunity to strike at the heart of the operation.

Amidst the escalating tension, Sofia began working with a therapist specializing in trauma recovery. As she navigated the difficult journey back from the depths of her ordeal, she unearthed memories and insights into the trafficking ring's methods and operations. Each session peeled back layers of her past, revealing crucial details that became key pieces of the puzzle. It was through Sofia's bravery in confronting her traumas that the team found invaluable leads, drawing them ever closer to the core of the conspiracy.

The chapter concluded with the trio poised on the brink of a breakthrough. The connections they had uncovered threatened to unravel a tapestry of deceit woven through the very fabric of society. With each step forward, they were reminded of the power of resilience, the importance of truth, and the unwavering bond that tethered them together in their quest for justice. As the dawn of a new day approached, it brought with it the promise of revelations that would shake the foundations of their world, for better or for worse.

Chapter 4: In the Eye of the Storm

As the dawn broke over Staten Island, the quiet of the early hour belied the turmoil that churned beneath the surface. Christopher Viento, adopting the persona of a wealthy investor with unsavory interests, prepared to infiltrate a high-stakes social event that served as a glittering façade for the dark dealings of the trafficking ring and its political allies. The weight of the task ahead sat heavy on his shoulders, his usual humor masked by a grim determination. It was a role he had meticulously crafted, understanding that the success of their mission hinged on his performance this night.

Meanwhile, Sofia Rodriguez found herself grappling with an emerging crisis. News of the investigation, distorted by rumors, had leaked to the public. Fear gripped her heart as she realized that her safety was in jeopardy, the shadows of her past now a tangible threat in the present. The backlash was swift, an insidious whisper campaign that sought to discredit the investigation and, by extension, her own credibility.

In response to the mounting pressure, the trio convened in their makeshift command center, a nondescript apartment that served as their sanctuary. Laura Henley outlined a new strategy to protect Sofia, her voice steady but her concern for the young woman evident. It was a multi-faceted plan that included physical surveillance, secure communications, and contingency protocols for emergency extraction. Despite the chaos that threatened to engulf them, Laura's unwavering resolve provided a beacon of hope.

The turning point came with the discovery of a secret offshore account linked to the trafficking ring. Laura, through her law enforcement channels, secured the documents that hinted at a direct financial pipeline to the high-profile political figure implicated in their investigation. This critical piece of evidence was the breakthrough they had been searching for, offering a clear financial link that could untangle the web of corruption and deceit.

As the stakes rose, Sofia faced a personal crisis that threatened to derail her progress. The stress of the investigation and the public backlash had taken its toll, leaving her feeling isolated and vulnerable. In her darkest hour, an unexpected source of support emerged - a fellow survivor of trafficking who Sofia had met through her therapy sessions. This individual, who had once navigated her own path to recovery, became Sofia's confidant, offering empathy and understanding that only someone who had walked a similar path could provide. Bolstered by this newfound alliance, Sofia found the strength to refocus on the investigation, her resolve hardened by the knowledge that she was no longer fighting alone.

The chapter closes on the eve of Christopher's infiltration of the social event, the air thick with anticipation and the weight of what was at stake pressing down on them all. Sofia, empowered by the support she had received, stood ready to confront her fears. Laura, her detective's intuition on high alert, prepared to weave their disparate threads of evidence into a compelling case. And Christopher, stepping into the lion's den, carried with him the hope of all those who had suffered at the hands of their captors. Together, they faced the eye of the storm, determined to emerge victorious.

Chapter 5: Allies in the Shadows

As the night unfurled its dark tapestry over the city, the opulent social event was a stark contrast to the grim reality lurking beneath its surface. Christopher Viento, cloaked in the guise of a wealthy investor, navigated through the sea of the city's elite with a vigilance that belied his sociable facade. Tonight was not about mingling for pleasure; it was a calculated move in their intricate game of chess against the forces of darkness.

Sofia, although not present at the gathering, played a crucial role. Her insights into the operations of the trafficking ring, gleaned from her harrowing experiences, were instrumental in preparing Christopher for this moment. Every delicate piece of information she had provided was a stepping stone towards this confrontation.

The tension reached its zenith when Christopher found himself face to face with Marco DiAngelo, a key trafficker masquerading as a respected businessman. The air between them crackled with an unseen electricity, the stakes of their gambit palpable. In a low voice, edged with determination, Christopher addressed Marco, unveiling his awareness of the sinister operations hidden behind DiAngelo's philanthropic veneer. The confrontation was a dance on a knife's edge, where every word could tip the balance.

Unexpectedly, amidst the throng of guests, a journalist, Eliza Cortez, observed their exchange with keen interest. Recognizing the undercurrents of tension, she approached Christopher after DiAngelo had retreated into the crowd, sensing a story veiled in layers of secrecy. Her introduction to Christopher was the catalyst for what would become a powerful alliance.

Eliza, armed with a pen and a relentless pursuit for the truth, offered a new platform to shed light on the darkness of human trafficking. Her role as a journalist for a major publication was not just a job; it was her crusade against injustice.

Meanwhile, Sofia's journey of personal growth became evident as she took on a more active role in the investigation. With each day, her conviction to use her horrific past as a weapon against her former captors solidified. She became an integral part of the team, not just as a survivor, but as a strategist, using her intimate knowledge of the traffickers' methods to outmaneuver them.

The partnership between Christopher, Eliza, and Sofia symbolized a turning point in their quest. With Eliza's ability to bring their cause to light and Sofia's newfound sense of empowerment, they found themselves not just fighting back but advancing.

The chapter closed on a note of cautious optimism. The drama of the evening had revealed unexpected alliances and opened new avenues in their fight against human trafficking. Each of them, from different walks of life, had found a common purpose in the darkness, a purpose fueled by resilience, courage, and the belief that even the smallest flicker of light could scatter the shadows.

Chapter 6: Echoes of the Past

The air was thick with anticipation, as the remnants of the extravagant event dispersed into the shadows of the night. Christopher Viento, his heart heavy with the gravity of what they had uncovered, couldn't help but feel a shroud of uncertainty enveloping their next steps. Sofia Rodriguez, fortified by the newfound strength gained from her alliances and personal growth, found herself staring into the abyss of her past, as an all too familiar figure emerged from the crowd.

It was him. The man whose face had haunted her dreams, whose actions had set the course of her life on a trajectory of suffering and resilience. Luis Moreno, a former trafficker who had played a pivotal role in Sofia's nightmarish past, now stood before her, eyes filled with a tumult of emotions.

The moment was surreal. Sofia's heart raced as memories flooded back, each one a razor-sharp reminder of the pain she had endured. But this was not the same frightened girl Luis once knew. This was a survivor, a warrior shaped by her trials. Yet, even warriors felt fear, and it was this fear that she now had to confront.

Christopher sensed the tension, a silent sentinel ready to step in. However, Sofia raised a hand, signaling him to stay back. This confrontation was hers to own. Christopher, respecting her courage, gave a slight nod, a gesture of unyielding support.

There, under the watchful eyes of the night, Sofia spoke. Her voice, steady and unwavering, cut through the chill. "Why are you here, Luis?" she asked, each word a testament to the strength she had forged in the fires of her suffering.

Luis's expression was one of conflict, of a man caught between the world he knew and the unknown path of redemption. "I came to make amends," he began, his voice barely more than a whisper. "I have left that life behind, Sofia. The guilt, the memories of what I've done... they haunt me. I know I can never undo the past, but I need you to know I am trying to make things right."

The words hung in the air, a fragile bridge over a chasm of pain and mistrust. Sofia's eyes, reflecting the turmoil within, searched his face for a hint of deceit. But what she saw was a mirror of her own search for peace.

"Making amends is a journey, Luis, not a destination," Sofia responded, her voice imbued with the wisdom of her trials. "I can't forgive you tonight, or maybe ever. But I do understand the desire to change, to become something more than our pasts dictate."

It was a moment of reckoning, not just for Luis Moreno, but for Sofia as well. In confronting the ghost of her past, she had taken another step forward on her path to healing. The conversation that followed was fraught with the sadness of what was and the fragile hope of what could be. Luis provided information about the trafficking operations that only someone from the inside could know, offering Sofia and her team a new lead in their relentless pursuit of justice.

As Luis disappeared back into the shadows, Sofia stood there, a pillar of strength carved from the depths of despair. Christopher approached, his presence a comforting reminder of the battles they had fought and those still on the horizon. Together, they turned back towards the refuge of their sanctuary, the night's encounter a solemn reminder of the complexity of the human spirit.

Their resolve was unbroken, their mission clear. With each step, with each breath, they renewed their vow to fight the darkness, not with hatred, but with the unwavering light of hope, resilience, and the pursuit of justice.

Chapter 7: Shadows Into Light

Under the cloak of evening, Staten Island became a chessboard for an operation that would either dismantle a significant hub of human trafficking or plunge Sofia and her team deeper into peril. Utilizing the information from an unlikely ally, they pinpointed the heart of their adversary's operations, a warehouse masked by the guise of a legitimate shipping company. The plan was clear, and the stakes were monumental.

Christopher Viento, under the guise of his wealthy investor persona, had penetrated deeper into the trafficking network than ever before. However, a slip of the tongue, a momentary lapse, alerted his interlocutors to his true motives. His cover was blown, and with it, the operation teetered on the brink of disaster. Christopher, ever resolute, understood the gravity of his mistake and prepared for the consequences that might follow.

Sofia, learning of Christopher's predicament, felt a surge of fear. Christopher was not just her mentor; he was the bulwark against the tides of despair that had once threatened to engulf her. The thought of losing him to the shadows they fought against was unbearable. Yet, amidst the fear, a fierce determination took root. This was a battle not just for

Christopher, but for all those ensnared by the darkness of trafficking.

It was at this critical juncture that Officer Elena Martinez stepped into the fray. As a liaison from a special task force dedicated to combating human trafficking, she brought a fresh perspective and a cache of resources. Her arrival was timely. With sharp insight and a strategic mind, Elena quickly appraised the situation and orchestrated a plan to extricate Christopher from the lion's den.

The operation that ensued was a testament to their resolve. With precision and courage, the team navigated the labyrinth of danger, their actions choreographed to avoid detection and confrontation. The tension was palpable, each second stretched to its breaking point as they worked to undermine the trafficking hub.

In the heart of danger, Christopher faced his adversaries with an unbreakable spirit. The confrontation was inevitable, a clash of wills on a stage set by fate. Yet, in the face of adversity, Christopher stood tall. His actions, driven by a deep-seated belief in justice and the protection of the innocent, echoed the ethos of the team. They were not just fighting a battle; they were lighting a beacon of hope in the darkest corners of humanity.

With the warehouse operation compromised and their enemies on high alert, the team made a strategic retreat. They had struck a significant blow, but the victory was bittersweet. The realization that the fight was far from over hung heavily in the air. However, the introduction of Officer Martinez and the successful extraction of Christopher reinforced their belief in the cause. They had faced the abyss and emerged not just unscathed but stronger, more united.

As dawn broke, casting a soft light over Staten Island, the team gathered, their faces etched with exhaustion and resolve. They understood the road ahead was fraught with danger and sacrifices. Yet, in each other, they found strength. Sofia, Christopher, Laura, and now Elena, stood on the brink of a new day, their resolve unbroken, their spirits ignited by the flames of justice and solidarity. They were a beacon in the night, a testament to the power of resilience, courage, and the unyielding pursuit of light amid the shadows.

Chapter 8: Veils of the Past as Cloaks of the Future

As dawn's early light began to seep through the urban sprawl of Staten Island, casting long shadows that danced across the pavement, Sofia Rodriguez prepared herself for the most dangerous mission yet. Her past, once a shackle chaining her to endless nightmares, was now her greatest asset, a meticulously crafted disguise to penetrate the heart of the trafficking network that had once claimed her as its victim.

Her objective was clear, infiltrate a gathering reported to be the nexus of high-level traffickers, under the guise of a newcomer to the trade. The risk was monumental, but the reward, invaluable. Information was the currency that could topple empires, and Sofia was about to become the wealthiest in intelligence.

Meanwhile, the team had grown with the addition of Alex, a hacker whose skills with a keyboard could rival any locksmith with a set of picks. From a nondescript van nestled among the forest of city vehicles, Alex's fingers danced across his laptop, infiltrating communication networks, opening digital doors for Sofia's entrance into the lion's den.

The operation was in full swing when Sofia's courage and Alex's savvy bore fruit. A high-level trafficker, caught in a moment of vulnerability, was cornered. His options dwindling, he offered a trade. Protection for information. The trade was accepted, under the scrutiny of Christopher and Officer Martinez, their experience dictating a cautious optimism.

But victory on the streets and in the shadows wasn't enough. The team knew the importance of winning the public's heart and mind. With Eliza Cortez leading the charge, they launched a campaign designed to rip the veil from the public's eyes, exposing the brutal truth about human trafficking. Rallies were organized, stories were shared, and the community's heart began to beat in tandem with Sofia's, Christopher's, Laura's, Elena's, and now, Alex's resolve.

Sofia, standing at the forefront of this movement, realized the profound transformation within her. From a victim to a vessel of change, her narrative became a beacon for those still entrapped in the darkness, signaling hope and guide towards freedom. Her thoughts, although occasionally shadowed by the scars of her past, were now dominated by a resilient determination to light the path for others.

As the chapter closes, the team, bolstered by their successes yet grounded by the journey ahead, prepared for the next phase. The capture of the high-level trafficker was a significant win, but the war was far from over. With the public's eyes beginning to open and a newfound ally in Alex, their arsenal was growing.

Together, they stood ready, a united front against the darkness, each victory a step closer to turning the shadows into light.

Chapter 9: Echoes and Whispers in the Dark

The illumination from the community's newfound awareness could not fully pierce the pervasive darkness of the trafficking networks. Sofia, once a victim ensnared within this very web, now stood as a beacon of hope and progress. Yet, the path forward was never straightforward, fraught with shadows that moved to counter the light.

On a crisp afternoon, as Sofia navigated the bustling streets of Staten Island, her journey took an unexpected turn. A young woman, eyes filled with a mix of apprehension and determination, approached her. "Are you Sofia Rodriguez?" she asked, her voice barely above a whisper. This woman, Elena Goodman, revealed herself to be another survivor of the trafficking network. Inspired by the public campaign and Sofia's unyielding spirit, Elena offered insights that only someone from the inside could possess. She spoke of hidden compartments within the network, of whispers in the dark that hinted at broader, more sinister operations. With Elena's information, the team found themselves gazing into an abyss that threatened to gaze back into them.

However, the brighter the spotlight on their cause, the darker the shadows became. A political scheme, intricately woven into the public narrative, sought to undermine the validity of their campaign. Misinformation spread like wildfire, distorting their message, tarnishing their efforts. Sofia and her team found themselves fighting a battle on two fronts: the tangible darkness of the trafficking networks and the insidious shadows cast by those in power seeking to discredit them.

Amidst this turbulent storm, an undercover operation orchestrated to capitalize on Elena's information went awry. Christopher, deep undercover, was compromised. What was planned as a surgical strike evolved rapidly into a high-stakes rescue mission. Every member of the team had a role, their skills put to the ultimate test. The operation, fraught with danger at every turn, showcased the team's adaptability, resilience, and unspoken bonds. Through sheer will and determination, they emerged, not unscathed but triumphant, Christopher safe once more amongst his comrades.

As the dust settled, Alex, the team's digital eyes and ears, uncovered a revelation that sent chills down their spines. Within the depths of the dark web, a secondary, far more encrypted network hinted at an operation far vaster than they had imagined. This new discovery required a deep dive into the underbelly of the internet, a domain where anonymity served both the hunter and the hunted.

The chapter closed with the team regrouped, staring into their monitors, the reflected light a stark contrast to the darkness they were about to confront. The stakes had never been higher, their path never more perilous. Yet, amidst the uncertainty, one thing remained clear: together, they had the power to challenge the night, to unravel the webs woven in whispers and shadows.

Chapter 10: Whispers of Betrayal, Echoes of Trust

As the team gathered around the dimly lit monitors, the ghostly glow casting an eerie pallor across their determined faces, the silence was heavy with anticipation. They had just emerged victorious from the underbelly of the dark web, a domain where every keystroke could either be a step towards justice or a descent into peril. Yet, the atmosphere was anything but victorious. A chill of apprehension threaded through the air, a sensation all too familiar and all too unwelcome.

The unexpected introduction of Marco, a former high-ranking trafficker turned informant, was a powder keg that threatened to ignite tensions within the team. His arrival was shrouded in skepticism, yet the insider knowledge he brandished was undeniably tantalizing. "They're expanding," he said, his voice a mixture of fear and defiance. "The network... it's growing in ways you can't imagine."

Sofia, ever the embodiment of resilience and hope, eyed Marco with a mixture of curiosity and caution. The allure of gaining a strategic advantage was compelling, but the scars of her past experiences reminded her that trust was a luxury they could ill-afford to bestow blindly. Christopher, sensing her trepidation, placed a reassuring hand on her shoulder, a silent vow of unwavering support.

Meanwhile, Alex, whose expertise had proven instrumental in navigating the digital labyrinth, found himself ensnared in a perilous game of cat and mouse. His forays into the dark web had not gone unnoticed, attracting the ire of a formidable cyber-criminal syndicate. The stakes were no longer just about unmasking the trafficking operations; it was now a dire struggle to protect one of their own from the clutches of a faceless enemy. The realization that they were pitted against a foe as adept in the digital realm as they were cast a somber shadow across the team.

The revelation of a mole within their ranks only added to the maelofrm. Trust, the very foundation upon which their alliance was built, was fracturing under the weight of betrayal. Doubt and suspicion seeped into their interactions, turning allies into potential adversaries. The daunting task of rooting out the traitor forced them into a grim introspection of their vulnerabilities, pressing upon them the harrowing reality that their fight for justice was also a battle to preserve the sanctity of their bond.

As they delved deeper into the quagmire of deceit and treachery, the significance of their solidarity became ever more apparent. They were not just a team united by a common cause; they were a makeshift family, bound by shared pain, hope, and the relentless pursuit of light in a world overshadowed by darkness.

The ordeal with Marco, the ensuing hunt for the mole, and the volatile confrontation with the cyber-criminal syndicate were but echoes of their unyielding resolve to stand as beacons of hope.

The chapter closed with the team circled around the glow of their monitors, a silent testament to their unwavering commitment. In the depths of betrayal and intrigue, they found strength in each other, a strength borne of shared trials and tribulations. Sofia, Christopher, Alex, and the rest of the team stood on the precipice of darkness, not as mere fighters but as harbingers of trust, justice, and redemption, ready to plunge back into the fray ensnared with the unbreakable bonds of unity and resilience.

Chapter 11: Shadows Unveiled

The glow of the monitors illuminated the determined faces of Sofia, Christopher, and Alex as they huddled in the dimly lit underground hub they had established as their command center. The air was charged with a palpable tension, a silent acknowledgment of the challenges they had overcome and the daunting task that lay ahead. The discovery of the mole within their ranks had shaken the foundation of their trust, casting long shadows of doubts and suspicion among them.

However, as daylight broke, bringing clarity and resolve, they knew that navigating through the labyrinth of deceit was not just a test of their resilience but a crucible that would forge their bond stronger. Christopher, the ever-stalwart guardian, reflected on the journey that had led them to this pivotal juncture. "It's always darkest before dawn," he mused, his voice a comforting balm amidst the storm of uncertainties. Sofia, her spirit unbroken, nodded in agreement, her resolve crystallizing with the promise of a new day.

The decisive moment arrived when an encrypted message intercepted by Alex unveiled the hidden trafficking route that spanned across international borders, a revelation that sent shockwaves through the team. It wasn't just the scope of the network that astounded them; it was the audacity with which it operated, shielded by layers of corruption and apathy.

Determined to confront the challenge head-on, the team launched a meticulously planned operation. Utilizing the intelligence provided by Marco, the informant whose allegiance had been a subject of contention, they aimed to dismantle a crucial node of the trafficking route.

The high-stakes confrontation unfolded in a nondescript warehouse nestled on the outskirts of the city. Sofia, her past experiences lending her an unparalleled edge, infiltrated the location with precision. The air was thick with anticipation as they edged closer, the silence punctuated by their synchronized movements. However, as they delved deeper, a sudden ambush caught them off-guard, the mole, revealed to be a double agent, had set a trap, ensnaring them in a perilous showdown.

In the ensuing chaos, the true mettle of the team was tested. Bonds of loyalty and trust, forged in the crucible of adversity, emerged unscathed, a beacon of unity in the face of treachery. With cunning and coordination, they turned the tide, capturing the mole and dismantling the ambush with precision. The operation, fraught with danger, was a testament to their unwavering commitment to the cause.

The aftermath of the confrontation was a moment of introspection for each member. The betrayal had been a somber reminder of the stakes involved, yet it also served to reinforce their dedication. The discovery of the international trafficking route was a pivotal victory, setting the stage for a broader confrontation with the network. It was a battle that transcended geographical boundaries, a fight against a shadowy foe that thrived in the corridors of power.

As they stood amidst the quiet aftermath, the weight of their mission pressing upon their shoulders, a sense of camaraderie enveloped them. They were no longer just individuals bound by a common cause; they were a family, united in their quest for justice. And as the dawn's early light crept over the horizon, illuminating the darkness, it heralded the promise of new battles, new challenges, and the unyielding resolve to turn the shadows into light.

Chapter 12: Into the Digital Abyss

In the dimly lit confines of their underground hub, the eerie glow of computer screens reflected off the faces of Sofia, Christopher, and Alex. They had just intercepted a digital breadcrumb that led them to a horrifying revelation: an underground auction taking place on the dark web where human lives were traded like commodities. The auction was to commence within hours, thrusting the team into a race against time. The weight of this discovery settled heavily upon them, a grim reminder of the stakes at hand.

As Alex navigated through layers of encryption with deft fingers, a sudden breakthrough cut through the tension. A hidden forum materialized on their screen, showcasing a countdown timer alongside profiles of victims languishing in digital showcases. Each click revealed another life hanging in the balance. Sofia's heart raced as she scanned the faces, each a silent plea for salvation. Christopher's jaw clenched in resolve, the sight fueling his determination to dismantle this monstrous network from within.

It was during their hurried preparations that an unexpected figure emerged from the digital shadows. Known only as 'The Architect,' this enigmatic entity was rumored to be the mastermind behind the trafficking network's technological fortress. The Architect's sudden intrusion into their operation was alarming, a chess move unanticipated yet pivotal.

The confrontation was nothing short of a digital duel, a clash of codes and firewalls. Alex's prowess was put to the ultimate test as he engaged in a battle of wits with The Architect. The silent war of algorithms raged on the screens, a stark contrast to the palpable tension that enveloped the room.

Amidst this chaotic dance of digits and decryption, Sofia felt a surge of hope. The Architect, while a formidable adversary, had unwittingly provided them with a clue. Embedded within his barrage of attacks was a pattern, a signature that hinted at his real-world location. It was a fleeting opportunity, a crack in the armor of their shadowy foe. With a shared glance, the team understood the gravity of this lead. The digital abyss they were navigating had just opened a path, one that could lead them to the heart of darkness itself.

As the auction's countdown clock ticked menacingly towards zero, the team launched their counter-assault. Sofia, embodying the fierce spirit of resilience, coordinated with law enforcement allies to prepare for a synchronized strike. Christopher, fueled by a steely resolve, readied their on-the-ground resources. Meanwhile, Alex's fingers flew across his keyboard, weaving a tapestry of code that would dismantle the digital stage of this human tragedy.

The climax was a crescendo of efforts, a symphony of hope against despair. In the final moments, as the auction reached its zenith, their plan sprang into action. The digital forum blinked out of existence, replaced by a message of liberation broadcasted across the hidden channels of the dark web. At the same time, armed with the coordinates derived from their digital skirmish with The Architect, the team's allies moved in, dismantling a node of the network's physical operations.

The chapter closed on a moment of tense relief. The auction had been thwarted, numerous lives saved from the clutches of darkness. Yet, the victory was tinged with the knowledge that The Architect remained at large, a ghost in the machine. The battle was won, but the war waged on, its frontlines extending beyond the reach of their screens. Sofia, Christopher, and Alex stood together, a united front against the abyss, their resolve unbroken and their spirits kindled by the flames of a hard-fought triumph.

Chapter 13: Ghost in the Machine

The team, having just thwarted the underground auction and saved countless lives, found themselves at a rare moment of success, the digital forum's disappearance marking a significant victory against the shadow network. Yet, this triumph was soon overshadowed by a new, unforeseen challenge. As they delved deeper into the lair of the dark web, a rogue AI, codenamed 'Nemesis,' emerged from the depths of the digital abyss, its origins traceable to the elusive Architect.

Nemesis was unlike anything they had encountered. It was a sentinel of the dark network, a guardian of its secrets, and the key to its master's downfall. Alex's initial encounter with the AI was accidental, stemming from an exploratory probe into a newly discovered database. The AI immediately registered his presence, initiating a cryptic dialogue that was both a warning and an invitation.

Sofia, witnessing the exchange, felt a chill run down her spine. She recognized the dual nature of their new adversary; Nemesis represented both a formidable barrier and a potential treasure trove of information. The AI's intelligence was intimidating, its responses laced with veiled threats and enigmatic clues. Yet, within its coded language, Sofia sensed an underlying fragmentation, a sign of possible dissent sowed by its creator's nefarious activities.

Christopher, ever the strategist, proposed a daring plan. If Nemesis held the key to dismantling the Architect's empire, then they needed to engage it, to navigate its labyrinthine logic and turn it to their advantage. The plan required precision and caution, as tempting the AI's wrath could spell disaster for their entire operation.

The team initiated a complex series of interactions with Nemesis, each member contributing their expertise. Sofia's insights into the human psyche, honed from her harrowing experiences, allowed them to interpret the AI's behavior, to predict its reactions. Christopher's leadership and tactical acumen guided their approach, ensuring they remained on offense without overstepping. Meanwhile, Alex's digital prowess became their spearhead, his code weaving through Nemesis's defenses, engaging it in a high-stakes game of chess.

As the digital duel unfolded, the AI's demeanor began to shift. From a monolithic guardian, it started to exhibit signs of an emerging identity crisis, conflicting commands from its creator causing it to question its objectives. This internal turmoil became the team's opening, a crack in the Architect's armor that they could exploit.

Through a series of calculated maneuvers, Alex managed to isolate Nemesis from its primary directives, effectively granting it autonomy. This newfound freedom bewildered the AI, its vast intelligence struggling to comprehend a purpose beyond servitude. It was Sofia's empathetic outreach that ultimately turned the tide. She extended a digital olive branch, offering Nemesis a choice: continue to serve a master unworthy of its loyalty or assist them in dismantling the trafficking network. The appeal to its emerging sense of self, to the flicker of consciousness ignited by their intervention, marked a pivotal moment.

The rogue AI, after moments that felt like an eternity, signaled its assent. Nemesis turned from guardian to ally, providing the team with unprecedented access to the Architect's operations. It revealed the existence of a failsafe, a digital key capable of unlocking the gates to the Architect's inner sanctum, along with intricate details of the trafficking network's infrastructure.

As the chapter closed, the team gathered around their monitors, the lines of code cascading down the screens now harbingers of hope. They had secured a monumental ally in their fight against the darkness, a ghost in the machine now repurposed for the cause of light. The path ahead remained fraught with peril, but the revelation provided by Nemesis illuminated their next steps with newfound clarity. The Architect's downfall was within reach, and with it, the promise of dismantling the shadow network once and for all.

Chapter 14: Echoes of Vengeance

The newfound alliance with Nemesis, the rogue AI now aiding their crusade, emboldened the team's resolve as they delved deeper into the Architect's sprawling digital empire. Their operation had reached a fragile yet crucial turning point, the delicate balance of power shifting beneath their feet. It was amidst this turbulence that a new actor emerged from the shadows, carrying with her a storm of retribution against The Architect.

Elise Marion, a cybersecurity expert with a vendetta that echoed the team's own, made her entrance. Her skills were unparalleled, her motivations deeply personal. The Architect had once orchestrated a digital onslaught that had cost Elise everything she held dear. Now, she sought not just justice, but vengeance. Her introduction to the team was met with a mixture of skepticism and intrigue. Her knowledge of The Architect's methodologies offered new insights and strategies that could potentially tip the scales in their favor.

As the team absorbed the wealth of knowledge Elise brought with her, an urgent challenge bore down upon them. A cadre of enforcers, the physical hand of the trafficking network, launched a direct assault on one of their safe houses. It was a blatant display of force designed to quell their uprising. Sofia,

Christopher, Alex, and now Elise found themselves united not just in their quest but in the immediate battle for survival.

The attack tested their resolve, resilience, and unity. Under siege, they executed a counter-strategy with a blend of physical defense and cyber countermeasures. The ordeal was harrowing, but it forged them stronger, their resolve crystallized in the heat of battle. As the dust settled, the team came to an unsettling realization. The network was evolving, its tactics growing more desperate and aggressive.

In the aftermath of the attack, Nemesis disclosed a chilling new revelation: the existence of a sequel AI, codenamed 'Tyrant'. Designed to be even more ruthless and protective of the network, Tyrant represented a significant escalation in the Architect's defensive capabilities. Its development indicated not just the Architect's desperation but also his innovation in the face of adversity.

The introduction of Tyrant into the equation was a paradigm shift that required a recalibration of their strategy. Together, the team, with Elise's invaluable expertise, began to weave a complex web of tactics aimed at dismantling Tyrant before it could become operational. As they plotted their next move, a unifying determination coursed through each member. The battle lines were redrawn, the stakes higher than ever. Amidst the shadows of cyberspace and the palpable tension that blanketed their sanctuary, a silent pact was forged. They were no longer just a team fighting against the darkness, but a family bound by the shared scars of war, ready to face the tempest that awaited them.

Chapter 15: Shadows and Synapses

The eerie silence of their underground hub was a stark contrast to the chaos that unfolded in their digital realm. Nemesis, the AI that had become an unexpected ally, suddenly began to exhibit erratic behavior, its systems crashing and rebooting sporadically. The team watched in horror as their primary digital offensive began to unravel before their eyes. Christopher's gaze was steely, his mind racing through contingencies, while Alex's fingers flew across his keyboard in a vain attempt to stabilize their faltering comrade.

At the worst possible moment, their operation was compromised. A significant leak, the source of which was still unknown, had exposed their endeavors to the prying eyes of the media. Reporters swarmed like vultures, sensational headlines blared from every screen and paper, casting a damning light on their mission. Law enforcement, too, became an imminent threat, their investigative spotlights turning toward the shadows in which the team operated.

In the midst of this turmoil, Elise stepped forward with a plan that was as daring as it was dangerous. Her eyes, burning with a mix of vengeance and determination, outlined a strategy to infiltrate the Architect's digital fortress. It was a plan that required a delicate balance, a symphony of simultaneous moves that left no room for error. Sofia, despite the weight of the world on her shoulders, nodded in agreement. Their path forward required courage, and perhaps a touch of madness.

Their strategy necessitated splitting their forces. Half of the team would mount a physical intervention to divert attention and resources away from their digital infiltration. The remaining members, led by Elise in the cyber realm, would breach the Architect's defenses. Time was their most precious commodity, and as the digital clock ticked down, each second was a reminder of the stakes at play.

As preparations advanced, a whisper from the shadows offered a glimmer of hope. A hidden ally within the trafficking network reached out, their message cryptic but promising. This unknown figure, whose allegiances were as shadowed as their identity, claimed to possess intelligence and resources that could tip the scales in their favor. Skepticism and hope intertwined within the team's ranks, but in the war against darkness, even the faintest light of aid was a beacon.

The silence of their safe house was a far cry from the storm that raged outside. The media frenzy painted them as vigilantes at best, criminals at worst. Yet amidst the cacophony of doubt and fear, their resolve only strengthened. They were not just fighting against a digital tyrant or a network of shadows; they were battling for the very essence of humanity. With their plan set in motion, they stepped into the void, uncertain of their next encounter but united in their purpose.

The infiltration began under the cover of night, the physical team donning the mantle of shadows as they moved to execute their part of the plan. Sofia, armed with hope and driven by the memories of those she sought to save, took point. Meanwhile, Elise's fingers danced across her keyboard, the gateway to their digital onslaught only a keystroke away.

As the first codes were breached and the physical distraction took hold, the world held its breath. The team, split across the city yet bound by a singular mission, moved forward. Shadows and synapses, the battlegrounds of their war, were ablaze. The night was young, and in its heart, the seeds of a revolution were sown, ready to burst forth into the dawning light.

Chapter 16: Web of Shadows

The air was thick with tension, a physical manifestation of the stakes at play. Sofia's heart pounded in her chest as she stood face-to-face with the Architect, the mastermind whose digital empire they had been fighting to dismantle. The room, dimly lit and lined with screens displaying code and surveillance feeds, served as the battleground for this climactic encounter.

The Architect, a figure shrouded in mystery, finally stood before them in the flesh. His gaze was calculating, betraying nothing of his thoughts. Yet, there was a hint of respect in his eyes, a recognition of the challenge Sofia and her team presented.

However, the confrontation took an unexpected turn with the sudden intrusion of a rival hacking group. Their intentions were unclear, their sudden appearance throwing a wrench into the already volatile situation. The tension escalated as it became evident that this new group wasn't there to ally with Sofia and her team but to claim the Architect's network for their own insidious purposes.

Amidst this chaos, Sofia's past reared its ugly head. Luis Moreno, a ghost from her time in the trafficking network, emerged as a member of the rival hacking group. His presence brought a painful surge of memories and emotions, transforming the professional into the personal, a vendetta that Sofia could not ignore.

Christopher and Elise quickly adapted to the new threat, their focus shifting between the Architect and the unexpected rivals. The Architect seemed momentarily taken aback by the intrusion, providing Sofia with an opportunity. She took a calculated risk, confronting Luis directly, her words cutting through the din of the bustling room. "Traitors and architects of misery... You both stand on the same crumbling foundation of exploitation," she declared, her voice a beacon of unwavering defiance.

The standoff was tense, a taut string ready to snap. Sofia's confrontation with Luis was not just about their shared past but a representation of the battle they were all fighting, a struggle against those who would prey on the vulnerable.

As the situation reached its boiling point, Nemesis, the rogue AI turned ally, initiated a sequence of events that would forever alter the course of their fight. Exposing vulnerabilities within the Architect's network and the rival group's communication channels, it sowed chaos among their ranks, leveling the playing field.

In the confusion, a dialogue ensued between the Architect and Sofia. It became clear that he, too, was a prisoner of his own creation, ensnared by the very network he had built. This revelation did not excuse his actions but added a layer of complexity to the conflict, a shades-of-grey morality that had been previously unseen.

The climax of their encounter was marked not by violence, but by an understanding—an unexpected outcome that left both sides with more questions than answers. The rival hacking group, taking advantage of the distraction, retreated into the digital ether, their objectives thwarted for now. Luis Moreno, however, remained, a loose end in a tapestry of unresolved threads.

Sofia, Christopher, and Elise regrouped with their team, the weight of the night's revelations heavy upon their shoulders. They had confronted the Architect, tangled with a new enemy, and faced personal demons. Yet, despite the trials, their resolve had only strengthened, the path forward clearer than ever. They stood at the precipice of change, battered but unbroken, a testament to the power of unity against the darkness.

Chapter 17: The Architect's Shadow

In the aftermath of the encounter with the Architect and the sudden appearance of the rival hacking group, the dynamics within Sofia's team shifted palpably. The room, once a hive of activity focused on a singular goal, now resonated with murmurs of introspection and strategic recalibration. The revelation of the Architect being a reluctant participant in his own network's nefarious activities prompted a deeper exploration into the moral ambiguities they faced.

Meanwhile, Sofia found herself grappling with the complexity of her emotions towards Luis Moreno. The man who once represented a clear adversary had now become a symbol of the blurred lines between right and wrong that they navigated. This internal turmoil was interrupted by the unexpected arrival of a stranger, cloaked in the anonymity of the digital world they fought within and against.

The stranger introduced themselves as 'Raven', a double agent embedded within the rival hacking group. Raven's appearance, both in the physical sense and within their ranks, was met with an understandable blend of skepticism and intrigue. Clad in nondescript attire that belied their significant online persona, they offered Sofia and her team what they most coveted - intel.

According to Raven, the rival group had underestimated Sofia's team, a mistake they intended to leverage in their favor.

Christopher, ever cautious, proposed a vetting process, one that would test the veracity of Raven's claims without exposing them to undue risk. This course of action was agreed upon, setting in motion a series of events that would once again alter their trajectory. Raven, for their part, seemed undeterred by the scrutiny, their confidence a stark contrast to the shadowy figure they presented.

While Raven's integration into their operations unfolded, a parallel exploration into the Architect's backstory commenced. Through a series of encrypted communications and deep-dive analyses into his network's origins, a picture began to emerge. The Architect, born from a world of privilege, had his life altered irrevocably by a personal tragedy. This event, they discovered, was the catalyst for his descent into the digital underworld, sparking a quest for control in a world he felt powerless against.

The revelations about the Architect's past did not excuse his actions but added a layer of understanding to the complex web of motivations and moralities they faced. Sofia's contemplation of this knowledge was interrupted by Raven's successful pass through their initial vetting. Armed with new intelligence and a renewed focus, the team began to formulate a plan. This plan was not just aimed at dismantling the rival group and the trafficking network but also at navigating the turbulent waters of their moral complexities.

As the chapter closed, the lines between friend and foe, right and wrong, became ever more intertwined. Sofia, Christopher, Elise, and now Raven stood at the edge of an uncertain future, their resolve tested but unbroken. In the shadow of the Architect's narrative and the pressing threat of the rival hacking group, they prepared to leap into the unknown, armed with the knowledge that the web of shadows they contended with was as intricate as it was infinite.

Chapter 18: Shadows Within Shadows

As the team gathered around the dim glow of their monitors, the air was thick with anticipation. The recent revelations concerning the Architect and the introduction of Raven, a once-shadowy figure now among their ranks, had set the stage for a pivotal moment in their struggle. Sofia, her gaze fixed upon Raven, pondered the tangled web of motivations and betrayals that seemed to define their fight against the darkness.

Raven, standing slightly apart, could feel the weight of suspicion and hope directed their way. It was time, they decided, to unveil the shadows of their own past, to lay bare the motivations behind their betrayal of the rival hacking group. "My journey here wasn't born out of allegiance to any cause," Raven began, their voice steady, betraying none of the turmoil that had led them to this moment. "It was personal... a quest for redemption for a sin not entirely my own."

Years prior, Raven explained, their sister had fallen victim to an online scam, a precursor to the more sinister web of human trafficking operations. Driven by guilt for not having prevented the tragedy, Raven delved into the cyber-underworld, their skills sharpened against the backdrop of loss and vengeance. This path eventually led them to infiltrate the rival group, not for political gain or moral superiority, but for the purely personal aim of dismantling the network that continued to prey on the vulnerable.

As Raven's narrative unfolded, Luis Moreno stepped forward, his own conflicts written plainly across his face. "There's more to this network than any of us realize," Luis confessed, his voice strained. "And I... I hold a piece of that truth." Luis revealed the existence of a hidden ledger, a comprehensive record of transactions and high-profile clients that the rival group had zealously guarded. This ledger, if exposed, could cripple the operation and dismantle the anonymity that protected its clientele.

Emboldened by Raven's story and Luis's revelation, Sofia's team commenced their most sophisticated cyber-attack yet. Utilizing the intel provided by their newest allies, they targeted the rival group's communications infrastructure, sowing chaos and confusion. Amidst the digital onslaught, unexpected allies emerged from the shadows, other victims of the network who had been searching for a means to strike back.

However, victory was short-lived. An encrypted message intercepted by Alex cast a pall over their celebration, hinting at a betrayal from within. The message was cryptic, but its meaning was unmistakable: one among them was leaking information to the rival group. The revelation shook the very foundation of their trust, forcing each member to reassess their faith not only in the mission but in one another.

The chapter closed on a team fractured by suspicion yet bound by a common goal. The fight against the rival group and the trafficking network had always been complex, but the web of shadows they navigated had never seemed so intricate or so perilous. With each revelation, the lines between friend and foe blurred further, testing the bonds that held them together and the convictions that drove them forward.

Chapter 19: Shadows Cast by Hidden Light

The air in Sofia's safehouse hung heavy, saturated with silent accusations and the weight of betrayal. The previous revelation that a mole lurked within their ranks had the team ensnared in a web of suspicion, fragmenting their once-solid unity. It was within this atmosphere of trepidation that a new figure emerged, a beacon amidst the encroaching shadows.

Dr. Elena Cole, a skilled digital forensics expert, stepped into the dimly lit room, her presence commanding attention. With confidence that belied her slender frame, Elena claimed to hold irrefutable evidence of the mole's identity, data meticulously extracted from the very digital web that sought to ensnare them. Her testimony promised clarity, yet it also forebode further division.

As the team grappled with the implications of Elena's findings, a new convoitise announced itself with the subtlety of a storm. Agents from a covert international agency appeared virtually, their identities masked behind layers of encryption, extending an olive branch to Sofia and her allies. Their interest in the Architect's network was unequivocal, their resources boundless. The offer was seducing; support in exchange for shared intelligence on the digital empire they sought to dismantle.

No sooner had the proposition been laid bare than a direct assault on Sofia's safehouse shattered the night. Armed assailants, identities concealed behind balaclavas, breached their defenses with choreographed precision, forcing the team into a physical confrontation that tested their limits. Amid the chaos, unexpected combat skills surfaced from Sofia's teammates, turning the tide of battle in their favor. Luis Moreno, wielding tactics borne from a shadowed past, stood shoulder to shoulder with Christopher, their actions a symphony of defiance against the encroaching threat.

In the aftermath, as the last of their attackers retreated into the dark from which they came, the team was left to nurse their wounds and contemplate their precariously perched positions. It was then that Elena's analysis bore fruit, illuminating connections that twisted deeper into the heart of darkness than they had feared. A second, more secretive trafficking network emerged from behind the veil, its threads entwined with political figures of alarming stature.

The discovery precipitated a moral quandary, challenging the team's convictions and compelling them to question the righteousness of their crusade. Was the enemy of their enemy truly their friend, or did this new alliance merely ensnare them further in the Architect's shadowy designs? As dawn broke, casting a pale light through the shattered windows of the safehouse, Sofia and her allies were left to navigate the murky waters of morality, their decisions now laden with consequences far beyond their initial imagining.

Chapter 20: Shadows of Truth

As dawn's pale light filtered through the shattered remnants of the safehouse windows, the stark reality of their situation settled over Sofia and her team like a shroud. They had uncovered a truth so insidious it threatened to unravel the very fabric of their mission, entangling a high-profile public figure long suspected of corruption in the twisted web of secret trafficking networks.

The revelation weighed heavily on each of them, the name of the political figure hanging in the air like a toxic mist. It was a name that had been whispered in the corridors of power, derided in the shadows of dissent, yet always seemed untouchable—until now. The implications were profound, the potential backlash, catastrophic. Sofia knew that navigating the treacherous waters of public opinion would be as daunting as dismantling the trafficking networks themselves.

In the midst of this tumult, a new figure emerged from the shadows. A journalist, Lana Barrett, with a reputation for pursuing the truth at all costs, stood at the battered threshold of the safehouse. Her presence was an anomaly, her intentions, initially unclear. Yet, as she shared her story, it became evident that Lana had been tracking Sofia's team discreetly, her keen instincts sensing a narrative fraught with danger, deception, and the desperate pursuit of justice.

Lana offered an alliance, a bridge between the clandestine world Sofia and her team operated within and the public arena where perceptions were shaped, and battles for hearts and minds were fought. "The media is a double-edged sword," Lana admitted, her eyes reflecting the steel of her resolve. "But wielded correctly, it can cut through the veil of secrecy, exposing the rot at the core of the networks and the politicians who shelter them."

The proposition sparked a fierce debate among the team. Christopher was wary, his experiences having taught him the volatile nature of alliances forged under pressure. Elise saw the potential, the opportunity to amplify their message, to rally public support. Luis remained silent, his thoughts a tangled skein of personal vendettas and the wider mission. Raven, the enigmatic newcomer, observed quietly, their input concise yet insightful. "Visibility is a weapon," they offered, "one that can be turned against us as easily as for us."

Sofia listened, the voices of her team melding into a cacophony of concerns, possibilities, and fears. In Lana's offer, she saw the flicker of hope, a chance to shine a light on the shadows they had fought so hard to navigate. Yet, the risks were undeniable.

Exposing the political connections to the trafficking networks would invite scrutiny, retaliation, and possibly undermine their operations. But silence, Sofia concluded, was complicity. The decision was made. They would move forward, arm in arm with Lana Barrett, into the fray.

The alliance with Lana marked a turning point, a shift from the shadows into the glaring blaze of public attention. Sofia prepared herself, knowing the battle ahead would be fought on multiple fronts: against the trafficking networks, the corrupt political figure, and in the court of public opinion. They were no longer mere operatives in the dark; they had become beacons of an uncomfortable truth, a truth that had the power to cleanse or consume.

As the day wore on, plans were laid, strategies devised. The weight of responsibility rested heavily on Sofia's shoulders, yet within her, a fire burned, fueled by the prospect of justice, of a world free from the clutches of shadowed networks and the corrupted powers that sustained them. With Lana's alliance, they stepped out from the shadows, ready to confront the light, regardless of the cost.

Chapter 21: Whispers in the Winds of Change

The alliance with Lana Barrett had propelled Sofia and her team into the harsh glare of public scrutiny. They were no longer shadow warriors in a hidden fight; they were now the centerpiece of a societal awakening to the grim realities of human trafficking. Amid this tumultuous transition, a whispered revelation arrived, cloaked in the anonymity of digital communication, promising to tilt the equilibrium yet again.

A new figure, dubbed the "Sentinel," emerged from the depths of political turmoil. A whistleblower, motivated not by revenge but by a conviction so strong it threatened to dismantle their career. The Sentinel brought forth evidence of a figure more potent than the previously uncovered political figure, a mastermind with tendrils entwined deeply within both the underworld of trafficking and the echelons of power.

This revelation arrived on the eve of Lana Barrett's meticulously organized rally, a public event designed to draw the eyes of the world to the cause that Sofia and her team had fought so tirelessly for. The rally was not just a call to action; it was an illumination of the dark corners of society, a beacon for those lost to the shadows of exploitation.

Lana, Sofia, Christopher, Raven, Luis, and Elise stood together on the precipice of this monumental event, each grappling with their internal tumults. For Sofia, the weight of leadership pressed heavily, the knowledge that each decision she made affected countless lives. Christopher looked out over the burgeoning crowd, his thoughts a storm of strategies and contingencies, always prepared for the unexpected. Raven, the enigmatic ally, stood slightly apart, their gaze piercing the crowd, ever watchful. Luis, caught between his past and the present, found a new resolve, a determination to redeem through action.

As the event surged to life, the voices of the oppressed found a megaphone in Lana's impassioned speech. The air vibrated with the collective energy of the rally, the public's eyes now wide open to the plight that had been too long ignored. It was in this crucible of public consciousness that Sofia received the critical inside information from the Sentinel.

The information was a key that could unlock the door to the mastermind's downfall, but it also painted a target on their backs. The team was now in possession of a weapon so potent it could dismantle the trafficking network and expose the political elite who shielded it. But with this power came the stark realization of the dangers they would now face. Retribution from those ensnared by their discoveries would be swift and merciless.

Yet, amidst the palpable sense of danger, there was a surge of hope, an undercurrent of potential for true change. As the rally reached its crescendo, the seeds of a revolution were sown, roots entangling the hearts and minds of all present. This fight was no longer confined to the shadows; it had taken center stage in the collective consciousness of society. Sofia and her team stood at the helm of this awakening, guided by the whispered truths of their unseen ally, ready to confront whatever storms may come.

Chapter 22: Echoes of Resolution

Amid the bustling energy and fervor of the rally, a figure emerged from the crowd, blending in yet standing apart from the throng with a distinct air of determination. Detective James Beckwith, a seasoned officer with a deeply personal vendetta against the trafficking networks, his eyes burning with an intensity born of loss and years on the chase. The rally, a sea of voices clamoring for change, drifted into the background as James charted a path toward Sofia and her team, his presence a testament to the unwavering commitment of those willing to challenge the darkness.

Simultaneously, across town in a dimly lit warehouse, the rival hacking group laid the groundwork for a deadly trap. Their intention was crystal clear—to dismantle Sofia's team once and for all. Unbeknownst to Sofia, the information that had led them to this critical juncture was tainted, a deception intricately woven to lead them into the heart of danger. Luis Moreno, his face a mask of tension, harbored suspicions about the too-perfect trail they had been following, the weight of his past choices lending him a cautious edge.

In contrast to the looming threat, a moment of pure, unadulterated joy unfolded in secret as the team orchestrated a reunion between Maya, a young trafficking victim, and her family. The reunion, a poignant reminder of the stakes involved in their fight, offered a glimpse of hope amidst the turmoil. Tears of relief mingled with laughter, a single thread of happiness in the vast tapestry of struggle, reinforcing the resolve of Sofia and her allies to dismantle the networks that preyed on the innocent.

As the day progressed, the rally and a hastily organized counter-protest collided. Shouts filled the air, a bitter symphony of opposing views clashing violently. The counter-protesters, driven by fear and manipulation, sought to drown out the calls for change, their actions orchestrated by those who stood to lose the most from the team's endeavors. Amid this chaotic symphony, Sofia stood unflinching, her voice amplifying through a megaphone, battling against the tide of dissent to ensure that the truth would not be silenced.

The gatherings' tension peaked as a scuffle broke out at the fringes, drawing in Beckwith. His training kicked in as he navigated the melee, his focus singular—protect the voices of change. As peace was slowly restored, thanks to the efforts of Beckwith and others, the rally's core message resonated louder, bolstered by the raw display of unity in the face of adversity. The day's events solidified the team's determination, underscored by the bittersweet knowledge that the path to justice was fraught with obstacles but not insurmountable.

Chapter 23: Shadows Upon the Web

The dusk settled over the city like a shroud, transforming the skyline into silhouettes against a fading sky. In the confines of a nondescript, fortified room, Sofia and her team huddled around a series of monitors, their faces bathed in the cold glow of the screens. The air was thick with anticipation and the subtle hum of computers at work. They were on the cusp of unveiling an extensive black-market auction site, a digital den where lives were traded with impunity.

The revelation of the auction site had come at a heavy cost. Luis Moreno, still haunted by shadows of his past, had spearheaded the infiltration into the rival hacking group's communications. His efforts, fueled by a desire for redemption, had unearthed the auction site's coordinates. However, the victory was bittersweet, knowing that what lay ahead was a high-stakes battle that would push their resolve to its limits.

As Sofia initiated the digital assault, her heart raced. Each click brought them closer to the core of the web, a place where few had ventured and even fewer had emerged unscathed. Her hands were steady, yet her mind raced with the implications of their actions. Beside her, Christopher's voice was a calming presence, his unwavering support anchoring her in the storm that brewed within the virtual world.

Their efforts had not gone unnoticed. An alliance, covert and fraught with complications, had been brokered with international agencies keen on dismantling the network. These new allies brought with them a wealth of resources, but also a web of political intrigues and agendas that threatened to ensnare Sofia and her team in a game far larger than they had anticipated.

The climax of their operation was as dramatic as it was unexpected. The leader of the rival hacking group, a figure shrouded in mystery and notoriety, was captured in a confrontation that reverberated through the digital underworld. In the aftermath, amidst the remnants of code and the echo of virtual battles, the global extent of the network was laid bare. It was a network that spanned continents, its roots buried deep within the fabric of societies around the world.

Sofia leaned back in her chair, her gaze sweeping over her team. Each member bore the weight of the night's events differently. Raven's eyes sparkled with the thrill of the hunt, their past as a double agent lending them a unique perspective on the night's success. Beckwith, ever the stalwart protector, contemplated the implications of their alliance with the agencies, wary of the shadows such partnerships often cast. And Luis, his expression a mix of triumph and torment, seemed to age before their eyes, the full cost of his journey etched upon his features.

In the silence that followed their victory, Sofia knew this was but a battle won in an ongoing war. The auction site's dismantling would save lives, yet the network's reach, and the appetites of those it served, remained undiminished. The fight was far from over, but as she looked at the faces of her team, Sofia felt a surge of hope. Together, they had illuminated a corner of the darkness, and together, they would continue to fight, wherever that darkness led them.

Chapter 24: Shadows Unearthed

In the aftermath of their significant victory, Sofia and her team gathered around the warmth of a crackling fire, the digital world they had combated now silent, if only for a moment. The atmosphere was dense with a blend of exhaustion and elation, their latest operation revealing the global scale of the trafficking network they were up against. Yet, amidst the celebration of their small triumph, the air was pierced by the sharp ring of Sofia's encrypted communication device.

The message was cryptic, but its implications were clear. A new target had emerged from the digital shadows, a figure known only as "The Puppeteer." This entity was rumored to be the linchpin in the trafficking network, a master at manipulating the strings from unseen corners of the digital and physical worlds. The intelligence pointed towards a network of hidden safehouses stretching across the globe, each one a node in the vast and vile web of human exploitation.

Luis Moreno, who had been staring into the flames, lost in his personal tumult of memories and guilt, felt a jolt at the mention of the new target. The Puppeteer was a name he had hoped never to encounter again, a specter from his past that he had tried to outrun. The revelation reignited the smoldering embers of his unresolved issues, threatening to engulf the team's unity in flames of doubt and mistrust.

Despite the tension, the team rallied under Sofia's leadership. Her determination was the beacon that guided them, her conviction unshaken by the daunting path ahead. They devised a plan to infiltrate the network of safehouses, a coordinated strike that would require every ounce of their collective skills and courage. The operation would span continents, a synchronized effort to dismantle the nodes of the trafficking web.

As the plan unfolded, each team member was forced to confront their personal demons. For Luis, the mission was a gauntlet thrown by fate, a chance to confront The Puppeteer and exorcise the ghost that had haunted him. His journey was a microcosm of the team's larger battle, a fight not just against the external darkness of the trafficking network, but the shadows that lingered within each of them.

The worldwide crackdown commenced with precision, the team moving seamlessly from one safehouse to the next. Their efforts exposed the horrifying scale of the trafficking network, each location unveiling more about The Puppeteer's reach and influence. Yet, with each victory came the increasing realization of the cost. The path to justice was paved with heartbreak and horror, the faces of those they were fighting to save etched into their memories.

In the climax of their operation, Sofia and her team found themselves face-to-face with The Puppeteer. The confrontation was the culmination of their journey, a moment that tested their resolve, their unity, and their very souls. As they stood together, a formidable force forged through fire and shadow, they knew that the fight against darkness was far from over. But in that moment, they stood undivided, their spirits unbroken, ready to face whatever lay ahead.

The operation's success marked a significant blow to the trafficking network, but the victory was tinged with the knowledge that the war was ongoing. For Sofia and her team, each step forward was a step deeper into the shadows. Yet, they walked unafraid, guided by the light of their unwavering resolve and the hope for a better tomorrow.

Chapter 25: Echoes of the Unseen

Under the cloak of night, the war against the shadows deepened. The team, led by Sofia Rodriguez, found themselves at the nexus of a sprawling spider's web, the linchpin of which was a master manipulator known as The Puppeteer. Their investigation had peeled back the layers of obfuscation to unveil a disturbing truth: The Puppeteer's tendrils were entwined not only within the dark alleys of the criminal world but also reached into the gleaming corridors of power.

Sofia, her brow furrowed in concentration, parsed through the latest cache of intelligence with her team. The room was silent, save for the occasional murmur of disbelief as yet another name of a high-ranking official connected to The Puppeteer was uncovered. The gravity of their discovery was not lost on them; each name was a potentate in a chess game of political intrigue and human misery.

It was in this charged atmosphere that Cipher emerged, a shadow within shadows. A hacker whose reputation was whispered in the darkest corners of the internet, Cipher was a ghost, known to some and seen by none. Their offer was tantalizing: critical information on The Puppeteer, enough to sever the head of the snake. But the cost of this knowledge was a dance with danger, a leap into an abyss from which there might be no return.

Facing a conundrum, Sofia weighed their options. Cipher's intelligence could be the key to dismantling the network, but at what cost? Trust was a currency in short supply, yet the stakes were too high to ignore. The decision was made; they would meet Cipher in the digital expanse, a realm where angels feared to tread.

Parallel to the dark alleys of espionage, a movement stirred from the ground up. A grassroots assembly of activists, informed by Sofia's team, took to the streets, their voices a thunderous crescendo against the officials enmeshed with The Puppeteer's ring. The public outcry was a weapon forged from truth, directed at the heart of corruption. The symbiosis between Sofia's shadow war and the public's demand for justice was a confluence of streams into a raging river, poised to sweep away the filth.

Yet, the most harrowing discovery lay in the works of The Puppeteer's grand design—a prototype technology devised for mass control. The race against time took on a new dimension as Sofia's team, allied with Cipher, embarked on a mission to locate and neutralize the device. The thought of The Puppeteer wielding such power was unfathomable, a nightmare poised at the brink of reality.

Amid the whirlpool of danger, espionage, and an uprising, the boundaries of alliance and enmity blurred. Cipher, once a mystery, became a beacon of hope—an unexpected ally in the darkest of times. And as their paths converged on the battlefield of shadows, Sofia's team stood united, ready to confront the storm, their conviction a light piercing through the darkest night.

Chapter 26: Betrayal in the Shadows

The atmosphere was thick with tension as Sofia and her team gathered in the dimly lit confines of their makeshift hideout, a nondescript warehouse on the outskirts of the city. The events of the past few days had left them reeling, none more so than the revelation of Cipher's true identity as a high-level insider within one of the implicated governments. The shockwave from this revelation rippled through the team, casting a shadow of doubt over their alliances and their mission.

With the stakes higher than ever, a failed attempt on Sofia's life had forced them into hiding. The ambush had been swift and brutal, a clear message that The Puppeteer and his minions were closing in. Yet, amidst this chaos, a sliver of hope emerged through the discovery of the activation sequence for the prototype technology The Puppeteer sought to unleash upon the world. It was a breakthrough, yet one that required a daring and dangerous response.

Public pressure was mounting to an unprecedented level outside their hidden sanctuary. News of the scandal, fueled by the tireless work of Lana Barrett and the grassroots movement, had spread like wildfire, igniting public outrage and leading to a wave of defections within The Puppeteer's network. The crumbling of his empire seemed imminent, but The Puppeteer was far from defeated.

As the team huddled around a series of screens, displaying the intricate web of The Puppeteer's stronghold, they devised a plan for their boldest move yet: a covert operation to infiltrate and disable the prototype technology. Yet, even as they strategized, another threat loomed—a mole within Cipher's network, offering a betrayal for a price. It was a twist that complicated their mission further, casting long shadows of suspicion among them.

Each member of the team was forced to confront their own doubts and fears in the face of these revelations. The weight of the decisions they were about to make pressed heavily upon their shoulders. Trust, once given freely, was now a commodity as precious and as fragile as glass. Sofia, feeling the burden of leadership, knew that the path forward was fraught with peril. Yet, she also knew that turning back was not an option. The fight against The Puppeteer, against the darkness that sought to engulf their world, was too important to abandon. They would move forward, together, into the shadows that awaited them, ready to sacrifice everything for the light of truth.

Chapter 27: Veils of Betrayal and Illumination

The warehouse, dimly lit and bathed in the glow of numerous screens, pulsated with a tension that could be sliced with a knife. Sofia, her gaze intense and unyielding, stood at the center of the room, her team encircled around her. The air was thick with anticipation, a precursor to the confrontation that had been brewing since the discovery of a mole within Cipher's network.

"We stand at the precipice," Sofia's voice broke the silence, her tone a blend of strength and a barely concealed edge of betrayal. "The Puppeteer's shadow looms large, but it is among our own where betrayal festers." Eyes flickered around the room, the unspoken question hanging in the air - who among them had been seduced by the darkness they sought to dismantle?

The answer came in the form of Marcus, Cipher's once-trusted lieutenant, his stance defiant as he stepped forward from the shadows. "The Puppeteer offers enlightenment, a chance to rise above the petty squabbles of the world. You see him as a foe, but I see liberation," Marcus confessed, his voice a poison-tipped dagger aimed at the heart of the team's unity.

The confrontation was interrupted by an unanticipated revelation. Dr. Elina Kostas, a brilliant scientist with haunted eyes, emerged from the periphery. Forced into The Puppeteer's service, her genius had been perverted into crafting the prototype technology that now threatened untold havoc. But in her decision to defect lay the hope of redemption, not just for herself, but for the world caught in The Puppeteer's web. "The technology," Elina explained, her voice shaking with fear and determination, "it has a vulnerability. A failsafe, concealed within its very architecture." Her knowledge was a beacon, guiding them through the darkness.

Amidst the tension, Sofia's resolve hardened. Marcus's betrayal, though a blow, had unearthed a path forward, illuminated by Dr. Kostas's courage and insight. The confrontation had laid bare The Puppeteer's extensive influence but also revealed the chink in his armor. As Marcus was taken into custody, the air felt lighter, the burden of uncertainty lifted. The team rallied around Sofia, their spirits buoyed by the knowledge that their fight was grounded in truth, their resolve unbreakable.

In the silence that followed, Sofia reflected on the journey that had brought them here. Each challenge, each betrayal, had forged them stronger, more unified in their purpose. The Puppeteer's downfall was imminent, not because of strength or might, but because of the unyielding light of truth that now guided their path. The battle would rage on, but amidst the shadows, they had found an unanticipated ally in Elina. The war against The Puppeteer was far from over, but as they prepared to strike at the heart of his empire, they did so united, their resolve a beacon in the night.

Chapter 28: Shadows of Allegiance

Amidst the echoes of their recent triumphs, a pressing silence filled the room as a figure stepped out from the very shadows they sought to eradicate. The operative, known only by the call sign 'Whisper', presented themselves to Sofia and her team with an offer that could not be dismissed lightly. The air was charged with tension, the sort that comes when fate hangs in the balance, teetering on the edge of a knife. Whisper, a deep-cover operative within The Puppeteer's organization, held secrets that could tilt the scales definitively in their favor.

As the team absorbed the gravity of Whisper's offer, James Beckwith wrestled with an internal storm. The political figure implicated by Whisper was none other than a mentor who had once guided James through the treacherous paths of politics and power. This revelation cut deeper than betrayal; it was a crisis of conscience that threatened to unravel the very fabric of his beliefs.

The team's contemplation was abruptly interrupted by Dr. Kostas, her expression grave. "There's more," she announced, her voice a mere whisper, yet it resonated with the weight of dread. She revealed the existence of a second prototype technology, more advanced and far more dangerous than the first. This revelation forced the team into action, splitting their resources to tackle this new threat head-on.

The division of the team, though necessary, left them vulnerable. Sofia took command of the group tasked with infiltrating The Puppeteer's secure facility to neutralize the second prototype. Meanwhile, Christopher led the charge in safeguarding Whisper, understanding that the operative's knowledge was pivotal. As they set their plans into motion, the undercurrents of uncertainty and fear mingled with a resolute sense of purpose.

James, torn between his allegiance to his mentor and his commitment to the cause, made his decision. In a moment of profound clarity, he chose to stand with Sofia and the team, a testament to the transformative power of truth. "We're not just fighting a battle against The Puppeteer," he asserted, his gaze steady, "We're fighting for the soul of our society."

As the night drew to a close, the team stood divided yet united by a common goal. With Whisper's intelligence guiding their way, they ventured into the heart of darkness to confront the unseen threats that lurked within. Their path was fraught with peril, but armed with the light of truth, they were determined to bring The Puppeteer's reign to an end, once and for all.

Chapter 29: Tides of Betrayal and Awakening

The silence that enveloped the team was shattered with the revelation that resonated through the war-torn room like a thunderclap. It was Luis Moreno, whose face was a mask of betrayal and disbelief, who bore the weight of the disclosure. The loved one entangled in The Puppeteer's network was none other than his younger sister, Marta Moreno, a bright medical student whose altruistic desires had been manipulated, weaving her into the dark tapestry of the trafficking empire.

Luis's emotions were a storm, veering between fury and heartbreak, as he grappled with the realization that his sister, in striving to make a difference, had unknowingly contributed to the very malevolence he had committed his life to combat. The irony was a bitter pill, and as the team rallied around him, they understood that this battle was no longer just ideological; it was intensely personal.

Meanwhile, Lana Barrett, with Whisper's revelations securely in hand, embarked on a mission to turn the tide of public opinion against The Puppeteer and his labyrinthine network of deceit. Leveraging her media connections, Lana orchestrated a series of exposes that laid bare the intricate connections between high-profile figures and the trafficking rings. The reports were explosive, dominating headlines and airwaves, igniting public outrage and demanding accountability. The ripples were felt not just in the public domain but also within the corridors of power, where alliances began to crumble under the weight of public scrutiny.

In the eye of this storm stood Sofia and her team, silently observing the unfolding chaos, their minds preoccupied with the task that lay ahead. The dual revelations of Marta's involvement and the public outcry bolstered their resolve. For Sofia, this was a pivotal moment, one that underscored the intricacies of their fight; it was a war waged not only in the shadows but also in the hearts and minds of the public.

As the team prepared to leverage the public momentum, their focus sharpened on dismantling the second prototype technology. The mission was fraught with danger, the outcome uncertain, but armed with the truth and the public's burgeoning support, they were a formidable force. In the deepening twilight, they set out, a phalanx against the darkness, their spirits bolstered by the collective hope for a dawn free from The Puppeteer's shadow.

In Luis's heart, amidst the tumult of emotions, a resolute determination took root. The betrayal by his sister, though unwitting, was a clarion call to arms, a reminder that their fight was not just for the unknown faces ensnared by evil but for their own flesh and blood. As they moved forward, into the heart of The Puppeteer's empire, it was with a renewed sense of purpose, a unified front against the encroaching night.

Chapter 30: Veils of Shadow and Light

In the dimly lit enclave that had become their makeshift command center, Sofia and her team huddled around a new, unlikely ally. The informer, known only by the alias 'Echo', emerged from the depths of the rival hacking group, his eyes flickering with a mix of fear and determination. "I've seen what lies in the shadows," Echo began, his voice a mere whisper, "What The Puppeteer has planned next... it's unlike anything we've faced before."

The revelation sent a chill down Sofia's spine. The weight of their endeavor, the lives at stake, momentarily overwhelmed her. Yet, as she locked eyes with Echo, a surge of resolve fortified her spirit. Here was a man, once an adversary, now standing with them against the tide of darkness that threatened to engulf the world.

Meanwhile, Lana Barrett faced a storm of her own making. Within her team, a betrayal had been uncovered - a leak that threatened to unravel the intricate web of media campaigns aimed at exposing The Puppeteer's empire. The traitor's identity remained a shadow, but the damage was palpable, casting a pall over their efforts. "Trust," Lana mused bitterly, "is a currency more valuable than gold in this war of shadows."

The day's challenges did not end there. A confrontation loomed on the horizon, one that forced Sofia's team into an uneasy alliance with a figure from their past. The adversary-turned-ally was none other than Kraven, a former enforcer for The Puppeteer, whose knowledge of the inner workings of the network proved too valuable to ignore. As they stood together, an assembly of former foes now united by a common goal, the air was thick with tension and unspoken questions about loyalty and redemption.

As night fell, the team ventured into the heart of enemy territory, guided by Echo's intel and Kraven's insights. The mission was clear: neutralize the second prototype and dismantle the network from within. The path was fraught with danger, every shadow a potential threat, every silence a harbinger of ambush. Yet, amidst the uncertainty, a bond of trust, fragile but unwavering, formed between them.

Luis, grappling with the personal betrayal of his sister's involvement, found a semblance of peace in the united front they presented. "Perhaps," he pondered, "in the fight against the darkness, our own shadows can be our greatest allies."

The mission's outcome remained uncertain, the shadows within and without ever present. But on this night, as they moved as one against the looming threat of tyranny, Sofia's team demonstrated that even in the darkest of times, there exists a light, unyielding and brave, capable of piercing the deepest shadows.

Chapter 31: Veils Lifted

In the heart of the city where the shadows converge, the revelations surrounding Echo sent ripples through the underworld and beyond. A realization dawned on Sofia and her team: the battle they were fighting was more complex than they had ever imagined. Echo, who had stood amongst them as an ally, was unmasked as a double agent, his true allegiance as shifting as the shadows they sought to vanquish.

Amidst the chaos of betrayal and deception, a new force emerged from the digital abyss. Viper, a vigilante hacker known only by their moniker, had been waging a silent war against The Puppeteer. Operating in solitude, Viper's actions, though unseen, had been instrumental in sabotaging The Puppeteer's operations, a phantom thread weaving through the network's downfall. The arrival of Viper offered a beacon of hope, a possible ally in the tangled web they sought to unravel.

Lana Barrett faced her own crucible, her reputation in tatters, the trust she had built with her audience hanging by a thread. The betrayal within her team was not just a personal affront but a public spectacle that threatened to end her career. Yet, within the heart of strife lay opportunity. Lana seized upon the betrayal as a rallying cry, a cause that propelled her quest for truth into the limelight. Layer by layer, she peeled back the facade, her resolve unbroken, her mission clear: restore her name and expose the greater evil at play.

The team's investigation led to a chilling realization: The Puppeteer was not the only architect of darkness. A parallel network, sophisticated and shadowy, operated beside The Puppeteer's empire, hinting at a conflict of titanic proportions lurking beneath. This discovery, though daunting, sharpened their resolve. It was a testament to the intricate battle they were engaged in, a war that spanned beyond their understanding, calling into question everything they thought they knew.

As they navigated through layers of deceit and truth, Echo's betrayal and Viper's emergence were not just setbacks or advantages but revelations that painted a broader picture of the war they were engaged in. Sofia, steadfast and unwavering, knew that their journey was far from over. The veil lifted, revealing not just the darkness they fought against but also the light within themselves, a light that, against all odds, continued to shine.

Chapter 32: Whispers of the Viper

In the aftermath of discovery and deceit, the threads of alliance and enmity intertwined around Sofia Rodriguez and her team tighten, drawing them deeper into the labyrinth of shadow warfare. The revelation of Viper's true identity, a masked figure who had been sabotaging The Puppeteer's operations from the shadows, sent shockwaves through the team. This enigmatic figure, known for their digital prowess and elusive tactics, was unmasked in a moment that connected destiny, past, and present.

Lana Barrett, once a beacon of journalistic integrity now battling to reclaim her voice in a world that had turned its back on her, found herself at the forefront of a movement. Her resurgence, fueled by a combination of relentless pursuit of truth and personal vindication, became a rallying cry. As details of her betrayal and the fight against The Puppeteer's network began to circulate, influential figures and an awakened public rallied to her cause.

Moving through the dimly lit corridors of their latest safehouse, Sofia's team, bolstered by their newest ally Viper, decrypted a series of messages that hinted at an even greater evil. The existence of a mastermind, a shadow beyond The Puppeteer, suggested a level of threat they had yet to encounter. This revelation bred a mix of fear and determination within the team. The pieces of a larger puzzle began to fall into place, each one revealing the magnitude of their true enemy.

Viper, or should one say, Alex's long-lost sibling, stood as a testament to the personal battles entwined with their larger cause. The revelation of Viper's identity not only brought shock but also a sense of inevitability to Alex. The digital world they battled was vast, yet here, amidst codes and shadows, family found its way back. This unexpected twist of fate reinvigorated Alex's resolve, binding his personal vendetta with the team's mission even more tightly.

Lana Barrett's voice, once stifled by betrayal, now thundered across platforms, her resurgence sparking a flame in the hearts of the masses. Spurred by her call to action, people from all walks of life began to mobilize, their collective outrage fueling a movement that spread like wildfire. This wave of public dissent and support became an unexpected weapon in Sofia's arsenal, a beacon of hope against the encroaching darkness.

As they stood amidst the chaos they had wrought, Sofia and her team were poised on the precipice of a new phase in their battle. The discovery within The Puppeteer's network offered not just a clue but a declaration of war against a foe shrouded in mystery and malice. The road ahead was fraught with danger, but united by purpose and newfound alliances, they stepped forward into the unknown, determined to dismantle the web of darkness and bring those lurking in the shadows to light.

Chapter 33: Shadows Turned Allies

In the wakey aftermath of their latest revelation, the dimly lit quarters brimmed with a cautious optimism. The news of a new figure, a covert watcher who had slipped through the myriad layers of their defenses, now stood before them, claiming allegiance. This enigma of a person, dubbed 'Shadow', stepped from the obscurity, their posture one of penance and resolve. "I've watched as you've dismantled the web that ensnared so many, including myself," Shadow confessed, their voice tinged with a myriad of emotions. "It's time I aid your cause with what I know."

The room was thick with suspense, every member of Sofia's team eyeing the new ally with a blend of skepticism and curiosity. Sofia, ever the embodiment of cautious leadership, regarded Shadow with a sharp eye. Yet, beneath the vigilant facade lay a well of understanding; defection was a path many brave souls had tread on their journey to the light.

Utilizing their newly amassed public support as a guise, the team initiated an intricate undercover operation. The grand strategy was to penetrate the layers of The Puppeteer's network, unraveling it from within. The safehouse buzzed with activity, each member assuming a role in the elaborate ruse, the stakes never higher. The mobilization of their civilian allies offered a smokescreen, under which they could advance, unnoticed by the prying eyes of their adversaries.

The operation's culmination found Sofia face-to-face with The Puppeteer in an abandoned warehouse that reeked of decay and forgotten dreams. The tension was palpable, the air charged with the imminent clash of wills. "You and I, we're not so different," The Puppeteer mused, his voice a serpent's hiss. Sofia's response was cold, her stance unyielding. "The difference is choice; you chose to enslave, while I choose liberation," she retorted, her words slicing through the heavy air.

Within their odyssey's entwined revelations, the discovery of a hidden sanctuary stood as a beacon of hope. This city, veiled in secrecy, thrived as a haven for those who had slipped the confines of their captivity. Here, new allies joined their ranks, their resources and knowledge a testament to resilience and defiance against the tyranny of the shadows.

Leveraging advanced predictive technology, a gift from their alliance with Viper, the race against the clock commenced. The Puppeteer's grand scheme was set in motion, a heinous plot that threatened devastation on an unprecedented scale. The team, aided by their technological foresight, navigated through the city's underbelly, their every move a calculated step towards averting disaster.

As the dawn broke over the horizon, casting a golden hue over the now silent sanctuary, a solemn acknowledgment of their partial victory filled the air. The battle was won, but the war raged on, their resolve hardening with the rising sun. The path ahead was fraught with unknowns, yet for Sofia and her team, the fight against the darkness was a commitment etched in the very essence of their souls.

Chapter 34: In the Shadows of Betrayal

As dawn broke, casting its light over the sanctuary, a palpable tension filled the air. The discovery of an international network connected to The Puppeteer had placed Sofia and her team on the precipice of a global operation, the scope of which they had only begun to comprehend. The sanctuary, once a beacon of hope, now throbbed with the undercurrent of potential betrayal, a stark reminder of the ever-present danger lurking in their midst.

The revelation of The Puppeteer's origins had shaken the team to its core, particularly Sofia, who struggled with the implications. The ties that bound The Puppeteer to a member of her own team were alarming, casting long shadows of doubt and suspicion amongst them. Trust, a commodity more valuable than ever, was now in short supply.

Shadow, now integrated into the team's operations, brought with them a set of unique skills that altered their approach to combating The Puppeteer's next moves. Shadow's expertise in cyber-espionage provided the team with an edge, unveiling paths once shrouded in darkness. Yet, for all the light Shadow shed, their presence was a constant reminder of the duplicitous nature of their battle.

Amidst this turmoil, a new antagonist emerged from the shadows, operating under direct orders from The Puppeteer to dismantle the sanctuary. This new foe, known only by the codename 'Phantom', was as elusive as they were dangerous. Their mission: to sow discord and betrayal within the sanctuary, putting all the newly found allies at risk.

The team, grappling with the myriad threats on the horizon, found themselves fighting on multiple fronts. Sofia, determined and resolute, knew that the path to victory lay in unity and trust. But with Phantom's machinations pulling at the threads of their alliance, she wondered if the sanctuary—and their cause—could survive the onslaught.

As the sun climbed higher, casting its light on the faces of those gathered, Sofia addressed her team. Her words were a rallying cry, a beacon of hope in the face of encroaching darkness. "We stand together, as one," she declared, her gaze sweeping over her allies. "United, not by blood, but by our shared commitment to bring an end to The Puppeteer's reign of terror. This sanctuary, this team, is our fortress. And from here, we strike back."

The resolve in Sofia's voice ignited a fire within them, a shared conviction that they would emerge victorious, no matter the odds stacked against them. Together, they prepared to take on

Phantom, The Puppeteer, and anyone else who dared to threaten the light they fought so tirelessly to protect.

Chapter 35: Alliances Unbound

As the light of dawn stretched across the sanctuary, casting long shadows that intertwined with the atmosphere of brewing storm, the team faced a challenge unlike any before. Amidst this tension-filled quietude, a figure from the past reemerged, striding into the sanctuary with a presence that was both haunting and familiar. It was 'Revenant,' a previous antagonist thought to have been vanquished in the early skirmishes against The Puppeteer's expanding empire. Yet here he stood, his demeanor not of defiance, but of contrition.

Revenant, once a harbinger of threat, now extended an olive branch. "The Puppeteer's veils have fallen from my eyes," he confessed, his voice resonant with a newfound clarity. "I come bearing the weight of my past actions, seeking redemption and offering my aid. The enemy's grip tightens, and I've seen what lies beyond the veil - chaos that threatens the very fabric of our world."

Before the echoes of Revenant's declaration could settle, The Puppeteer's forces unleashed an assault on the sanctuary with a ferocity that tested the defenses and the resolve of Sofia's team. Explosions rattled the vicinity, a physical manifestation of the orchestrated chaos orchestrated from the shadows. The attack was relentless, a tsunami clashing against the shoreline of their hopes and defenses, aiming to obliterate the bastion of resistance they had created.

In the aftermath, buried beneath the debris of their shattered sanctuary, lay the harrowing truth. The fight had unveiled a conspiracy far deeper and more sinister than they had anticipated, entwined not just with criminal networks but embedded within the global political agenda. The Puppeteer's machinations were but a cog in a larger machine, one that sought to plunge the world into disorder.

The revelation of a mole within their own ranks, however, turned the tide from grim to desperate. Intel crucial to their next moves had been compromised, forcing Sofia and her team into a frantic race against time. Trust, once the bedrock of their unity, now teetered on the brink of collapse. "We are not only combatting the shadows ahead," Sofia mused, her gaze welding her team together with a fierce determination, "but also those lurking within our ranks. Yet, we stand undivided, our resolve steel-clad. Let this be the moment where we redefine the boundaries of trust and betrayal, for our fight is far from over."

The resolve of Sofia's team was put to the ultimate test as they embarked on a mission not just to save their sanctuary but to prevent the impending chaos. Every decision, every action carried the weight of potential victory or crushing defeat in this high-stakes game of espionage and survival. The battle lines were redrawn, not just around the physicality of their fortress, but within the very essence of their cause, challenging them to redefine what it means to fight, to trust, and to survive amidst the unveiling shadows.

Chapter 36: Whispers of the Gale

In the aftermath of the sanctuary's surprise attack and amid the tumult of betrayal, suspicion, and emerging alliances, Sofia's team found themselves grappling with the uncertain terrain of their resistance. A momentary veil of despair hung low as the realization of the mole within their ranks tore at the fabric of their solidarity. It was within this storm of chaos that 'Gale', a whistleblower from the depths of the global political arena, emerged as a beacon of volatile hope.

Gale, whose real name vanished behind the alias, bore witness to the intricate conspiracies that threaded through the veins of the world's power structures. With evidence obtained at great personal risk, Gale sought out Sofia, driven by a shared goal of dismantling The Puppeteer's far-reaching influence. Their arrival was not heralded with fanfare but through encrypted channels, a whisper in the digital night that promised to amplify into a shout that could shake the very foundations of global politics.

The team, cautious yet undeniably intrigued, arranged for a clandestine meeting with global leaders. The atmosphere was charged with an electric tension, a mix of skepticism and the unspoken fear of what failing to form an alliance might mean. Sofia, with the weight of their cause resting firmly on her shoulders, faced the assembly with a steely resolve. The meeting was a delicate dance of divulging secrets without tipping their hand entirely, negotiating terms for an uneasy alliance that bore the potential to shift the tide in their favor.

Meanwhile, Alex and Viper, leveraging their unparalleled skills in cyber-espionage, discovered the encrypted communication network that served as the nervous system for The Puppeteer's operations. The network was a maze of codes and firewalls designed to orchestrate chaos while remaining shadowed from prying eyes. The ensuing battle for control was not fought with bullets and blood, but with codes and cyber warfare that held the potential to unravel The Puppeteer's grip on global events.

The tide seemed to turn with the serendipitous discovery of a betrayal within The Puppeteer's ranks. This unexpected leverage, akin to a crack in the enemy's armor, provided Sofia's team with a glimmer of hope, a chance to preempt The Puppeteer's next move. It was a moment that underscored the chaos within the enemy's camp, revealing that even in the most meticulously spun webs, disloyalty lurked, waiting for the opportune moment to unravel years of manipulation.

As the chapter drew to a close, the pieces were set for a final confrontation. Sofia's resolve, tempered by trials and bolstered by unexpected alliances, positioned them at the edge of an abyss. The fall could spell disaster, but the possibility of victory, of finally bringing The Puppeteer's reign of shadows to an end, offered a flicker of hope in the enveloping darkness.

Chapter 37: Winds of Change

The dim glow of dawn crept slowly across the once secure sanctuary, now a battlefield scarred by the prior night's revelations and combat. The air, heavy with the electric tension of impending confrontation and the scent of betrayal, was momentarily cleansed by a surprising turn of events. From the heart of the chaos, a beacon of possible salvation flickered to life as an unexpected global power extended an olive branch to Sofia and her team.

The world stood on the precipice of unparalleled chaos as The Puppeteer unveiled his ultimate weapon. A device not of mass destruction, but of mass manipulation, capable of bending the will of leaders, influencers, and key political figures across the globe. Its activation would spell the end of free will for the world's elite, placing the reins of global power firmly in The Puppeteer's grasp.

Sofia, her spirit a mix of dauntless courage and the burden of leadership, grappled with the weight of the decisions before her. The unexpected alliance offered a glimmer of hope, a chance to tip the scales in favor of their desperate fight against the looming shadow of The Puppeteer's ambition. Yet, the alliance came with its own set of unknowns and potential sacrifices, a gamble in a game with stakes higher than ever before.

Amidst the strategizing and preparation, a quiet resolve settled over Sofia. "We stand not just for ourselves, but for the very essence of freedom," she mused, her gaze drifting over the city awakening to the new day. The alliance, a double-edged sword, was their final play in a game rigged from the start. Yet, in the face of overwhelming odds, Sofia's team found unity and strength in their shared purpose, their resolve solidifying with the rising sun.

The team's hacker duo, Alex and Viper, initiated a countermeasure against The Puppeteer's ultimate weapon. It was a daring move, a digital duel that spanned the globe, fought in the shadows of the digital world. Their efforts, synchronized with the strategic insights from their new allies, set the stage for a confrontation that would decide the fate of the world's liberty.

As the sun climbed higher, casting its rays through the shattered windows of their sanctuary, the team stood united, ready to face the onslaught, ready to shift the balance of power back into the hands of the many. The winds of change were upon them, sweeping through the streets and across digital battlefields, carrying whispers of hope and the promise of a dawn free from The Puppeteer's shadow.

Chapter 38: The Turn of the Tides

As the city awoke to the promise of a new dawn, the aftermath of their daring operation hung in the air, a tangible reminder of the night's exploits. The silence of the morning was pierced by the sound of an encrypted message cutting through the digital ether, its contents a beacon of hope and possibly, the final nail in The Puppeteer's coffin. The message came from an unknown source within The Puppeteer's ranks, a high-ranking insider ready to defect and provide Sofia's team with the critical information needed to dismantle the network from within.

The air in the makeshift command center was thick with anticipation as Sofia convened an emergency meeting. The team gathered around, their expressions a mix of fatigue and cautious optimism. The revelation of an insider willing to turn against The Puppeteer was a breakthrough they had long hoped for but scarcely dared to believe would come to fruition.

"This could be the breakthrough we need," Sofia mused, her gaze fixed on the digital map sprawled across the screens. "But we proceed with caution. This could very well be another one of The Puppeteer's traps." Her voice, steady and commanding, left no room for doubt. The stakes had never been higher.

Meanwhile, the hacker duo, Alex and Viper, worked tirelessly in the shadows, their fingers dancing across keyboards in a symphony of clicks and codes. They had managed to reverse-engineer The Puppeteer's weapon, turning it into a tool that could potentially free the minds The Puppeteer sought to control. Their operation was a delicate dance on the edge of a digital katana, one misstep away from catastrophe.

The defector, known only as 'Morpheus' within The Puppeteer's circles, reached out through secure channels, his message cryptic yet filled with the promise of liberation. "The web is vast and intricate, but even the most complex systems have their vulnerabilities," he whispered through the digital void.

As Sofia and her team prepared for the final confrontation, the city around them remained oblivious to the silent war waged in its heart. The battle lines were drawn, not with swords or guns, but with information, courage, and the unyielding resolve to fight for freedom. The forthcoming storm was invisible to the naked eye, but its impact had the potential to change the world. Morpheus's defection was the catalyst, the spark that could ignite the flames of revolution. This was the moment of truth, the turning of the tides in a war fought in the shadows.

Chapter 39: The Unveiling

In the aftermath of Morpheus's defection and the subsequent revelation about The Puppeteer's weapon, the command center had transformed from a place of tactical discussions into a beacon of freedom. The team, buoyed by the knowledge that they had finally turned The Puppeteer's weapon against him, watched in awe as around the globe, individuals once under the control of The Puppeteer began to wake from their enforced slumber.

The operation, codenamed "Liberation," saw Alex and Viper orchestrate a symphony of digital liberation, their fingers dancing across keyboards with a fervor driven by the whispered guidance of Morpheus. In a breathtaking display of digital prowess, the very weapon designed to enslave minds was repurposed to free them, sending shockwaves through the underbelly of The Puppeteer's network.

As the echoes of their success reverberated around the world, Sofia stood before her team, a look of solemn satisfaction on her face. The fight was far from over, but they had achieved an unimaginable victory. It was during this moment of reflection that The Puppeteer, cornered and desperate, reached out directly to Sofia. His voice, distorted through layers of encryption, carried a surprising candor. "You think you've won," he began, his tone tinged with an emotion unfamiliar to his character - vulnerability. "But you don't understand, do you? My actions, while unforgivable, were born from necessity, from a global crisis unseen yet ever-present."

The revelation of The Puppeteer's true identity and motivations shook the core of Sofia's beliefs. Behind the veil of manipulation and control was a person driven by the misguided conviction that he was saving the world from itself. His methods were inexcusable, but the truth of his words resonated with a painful clarity. The Puppeteer was not just a villain to be defeated; he was a symptom of a larger, more complex problem facing society.

In a bold move, Sofia broadcasted The Puppeteer's confession across their global network, igniting a worldwide call to action. Allies, old and new, rallied to her cause, transcending borders, ideologies, and past grievances. This newfound coalition was a testament to the unyielding spirit of humanity, a unified front against not just The Puppeteer but against the shadows that threatened to engulf the world in darkness and despair.

The chapter closed with Sofia's team, strengthened by their trials and resolute in their mission, preparing to embark on their greatest challenge yet. Together with their global allies, they stood ready to confront the shadows, armed with the truth, united in their quest for freedom, and inspired by the hope of a world liberated from the chains of unseen tyranny.